FADING OUTSIDE

Don Schaeffer

ISBN: 978-81-19228-53-9

First Edition: 2023
Rs. 200/-

Cyberwit.net
HIG 45 Kaushambi Kunj, Kalindipuram
Allahabad - 211011 (U.P.) India
http://www.cyberwit.net
Tel: +(91) 9415091004
E-mail: info@cyberwit.net

Printed at Vcore.

Contents

The Joust

Poetry is still marketing,
even when you don't play for keeps.
The yes is worth 20 points.
The no answer may as well spell death.
It's so quiet in the land of reading.

You look at a face with no features.
You make up what the thoughts are.
The loneliness is a thrill of it's own.
It is really only a wish
that the blood in the words
does not leak in vain.

A thin fluid of words comes out,
largely an annoyance but with poison in it.
The value of it is an illusion, they all know.
The poem asks and waits while
the pages are delicately closed in treated paper.

Marianella The Regenerate

She is good at
gentility. I can tell
she was raised with it.
No one learns this
so quickly and
can enjoy it
through their youth.
I'm not arguing even
though I was never
granted that gift.
It is a gift whose joy
is in the giving and
in the hard path.
The hardship is
of a gifty kind, not
earned with tears. She
breaks through the world
with a smile that
can't be learned.

And Her Mother is a Bee

The bee lands on the dandilion
and walks on it in two small circles
first as the clock then counter.
The bee briefly takes to the air
and lands on another flower
first circling left then right
and taking off for another dandilion.

The bee repeates this work all afternoon
without a paycheck, legs lumped in boots
of wax. The bee circles ritually
exactly one time clockwise and then counter
from dandilion to dandilion,
showing no fatigue. The turning is with joy
as far as the unsympathetic eye can tell.
The bee achieves what she achieves
with be no clear blessing
then dies an early death.

The Cat at Two AM

I wonder why
she makes the growly sound.
Although she's small
and mine, she hides many secrets.
Not of my species,
related, but not quite close enough.

How much
can I depend on love?
Teeth and claws in the night,
she speaks a different kind of language
and makes odd aliances in the dark,
hiding in the forgotten corners.

Love is a mystery
in the vast vacuum of the night.
Her loyalty is not
tested enough. The new world
is made of secrets,
many unreadablem words,
many whispered warnings.

Two Views of Love

Before she died
she kissed him on his lips,
she took his hand
and placed it on her breast.
Before she died,
he made a scene,
insisting that she fight with God.
He left her in silence.

My Name

I ride a small pony
his name is Don.
We have had a very
coopeative agreement,
all my life. I get
carried about inside and out
I just shift my glance and
change the pointing of my vision
my eyes do the work of making pictures.

I would miss Don if
it should vanish.
I could survive,
but instructing the aimers
could get complicated.
The aimers, I presume,
have become very used to Don.
I know they agree,
although I have not
been informed.

And, of course,
I don't know what
would inform me.
The colors swirl around me
as things operate in coordination with
entities generated in my eyes
and the special relevance of music.

Watching a Man Grow Old

As far as I can tell
it's difference between the outside
and the in. We are partly blind to changes in ourselves
even if everyone else can see them.
We start to walk and talk differently,
unsually you can at least partly see that.
And time splits off into sections of
being here and not. We get partly
cut away, even while we seem to many
to be still alive. Death is part of growth.
It's segmented much the same.
You can keep your eyes as long as you don't close them.
Hope doesn't go away but the roadway to tomorrow
roughens. It's easy. One can see
how the list of places and paths to
love quickly narrow to the closing.

Reading a Passing Email

It's too late now
for everything, but
wishes are still fresh.
The visions have
wavy insistent arms.
I remember how
I used to entertain hope.
I never learned to
silence it: hope for impossible
conversions to love,
hope for conversion from
dream to fact. The arms
of my dreams still reach out
into vacuums.

What is a Microscope?

A microscope is a convenient glass wall
that protects me from the mystery of
what was, is, will be, the passing.
As it is, the glass creates an otherness,
a never, a safety net of
mechanics and light.

How the Pillow Goes

Yes, tonight is different.
I felt the rush of sleep enter my brain.
I only caught it before it
took away my will.
I felt
the firm, soft
fingers of sleep
before the pictures.
I learned
the face of sleep.

The Nutcracker

It was composed of order.
The stage was clean,
carefully arranged. The people
were ghosts of delight
who made magic with their fingers
and carried evolution in their lips.
They went beyond time. Their arms
were brighter than sunlight.
Their smiles defied category.
They nested their bodies gently,
releasing a glow as they moved.
They held memories dear.
They lived and laughed forever.

The Rules

I know it as
a neatly ordered room.
Justice is what
I expect. But what I find
is the human distortion of justice.
It may not be
the right planet for me.
I may have to
construct my own,
and populate it with clones.
Then I won't be angry.
I sit alone
writing my poetry
that doesn't find a page.
I make my thought
that doesn't find a poem.

Les Sylphides

They used to call it innocence.
The dream is one of those gentle ones
that doesn't want to frighten its maker,
especially while the protector of dreams is watching.

The dream slips quietly along
with a faint, kind smile, bending then lifting her head.
She is a big dream, unafraid and gentle,
creating waves of knowledge and science.

And no one doubts her.
They all need the dream too much,
and none wants it to die,
even as it fades.

The Adventure of Night

Life is a ghost story,
the kind that brings a giggle,
while alone, on my bed,

in the silence of night.
What is real and what illusion?
What is rumor and fancy?

All I know is the silence and darkness,
soil in which God plants dreams.
There are big truths hidden here,

spirits wearing masks
who whisper lies and rumors
but let slip pieces of restless truth.

The Voice

Out of the dark
a voice said,
"Do you know who that is?"
I swear
I was asleep then,
and when I opened my eyes
Francois, the cat
was looking down at me
from a perch on the pillow.
I could only greet her as I
greet the morning,
the first thanks of the day.
I did wonder who spoke,
but had no one to ask.
I let Wonder answer.

A Message in the Melody

Just as the music said it,
the day was calling for change,
an unsettling call, asking for

something that won't favor me.
And I don't know what,
having fallen into the uninformed class

with such direction not provided.
Just endure, the instruction assures.
Your needs have not been assessed.

Contact Sports

If you look
close-up
through a microscope at There is a system to it.
We (I use this pronoun advisedly)
the team, the couple, the fundamental grouping

the unity that keeps life. We
are the organization of the world.
There is nothing else but empty space.

With our hands and breasts and bodies,
we exist, for a time
before vanishing. All the sounds

that fill our minds, all the touches on our sleeves.
It is God. It is living prayer. When it
silences, we are gone. Silent morning never wakes.

Not the Eyes

It's the hands
not the eyes
that make us real.
what constitutes flesh,
the boxes that organize life
squeeze each other in life grips,
hug tight. Life wrestles.
Small cells make sad attempts
to gain against big ones.
Where do they get the
proclivity to gain?
How much do they
need to take the space?
The body is a contest,
each unit envious of its neighbors.

True Authority

The quiet ones
hold the secrets.
They don't boast,
they just give out honors.
Did you ever stroke
the soft back of a hero
and watch the honor in his eyes?
It is worth a million joys.
You can hear the honor
from the earth and watch the
deep supernatural smile:
the earth carrying
whispers and forgiveness.

The Creepy, Lonely Place

As my skin tightens
and dries, the night
grows a presence that
follows me into day.

I generate
words and phrases for myself
I never would have thought.
The room makes strange language

I sometimes understand.
I own myself less.
My ownership slips into strips.
I wear rags halfway.

Maybe I should be afraid.
I dread but it isn't fear.
We don't make the language
for things this big.

The Collection of Birthdays

I can feel the floor shake
as the army of years
takes a wide berth around me,

not wanting to be
caught too close.
I am much too frightening now.

My love is ugly and makes them
hide their eyes. I know I don't
watch them right with my

crooked face. I can't
call them nearer. I know
they will not come, won't even catch my eyes.

Password

I see how
I trap myself
every time I think
in my defense.
I don't even have to speak
and every speech tangles me
deeper in darkness.
I wound my case
with every word.
Where is the path out of this place?
The little tricks no longer seem to work.
So alone when no allies can defend me.
The worst sin is peace.

Ok. It is the people
on the other side of the screen
who most concern me.
It is the fantasy of fame.
I can stop
entertaining fantasies.
I can let that slip away
and just laugh and taste.
I can observe and understand.
The pain of this will not kill me.
It will just fade me as if
I put on my dressing gown.

The Fetish of Living

No one can do it right.
The method is precise and
the secrets are not published for
public view. But the general formula
is widely known and practiced
imperfectly by many. Imperfect practice
stirs the world. Incomplete response
and complicated wishes stir living.

The Inner Lute

This is the time of meanings,
secret codes, suddenly appearing
unexplained. This is a dark time
at the tippling edge of day.
Now I speculate about what I am seeing,
I link it to impossible theories.

This is a state we are warned about.
If anyone knew about this,
they would feel the danger.
I know the danger, the fear of it
rumbles in my mind.
Yet it gets more distinct
like the strumming of a lute.

A Coming to Know

Just before dawn,
in the deepest part of the night,
wonderful things are being said.
Standing on the table of night
where she's not allowed to be,
the animal tries to speak.
Her voice is deep and fearful.
I have not heard that reaching voice before.
She aspires, calls out.
I try to hold her. I can feel her
but can't get a grip to lift.
She makes a decision slowly,
leaps to the floor,
vanishes through the half opened door.

Ear Hands

When I approach the podium
I can see the restlessness
as an idea breathes. I know
how it will be embodied.
The air will lift the weight
in lobes of time. It will be
an invisible dance carried
by moving hands.
Only thin time will lift its weight.
None of us know how. But
as it emerges
some kind of eyes make bodies.

My Cat the Pope

Francoise won't come to me.
It's the second day.
I lost the authority of love.
That's the power
animals claim. They are
the officers granting the
honor of innocence.
I am judged by the powerful speaker
which proclaims judgment by
avoiding glances.

Biography

Pop the eyes come open.
It's the morning of the world.
Nothing is mine and
everything is mine.
There are no other claimants.
Then pop! No longer alone just
biggest and best. Slowly ownership
becomes chairmanship. Oh
it's difficult here as
pieces of godliness erode away
through personal wars until there's
mere membership.

I am not the master
but I am in the master's mind.
My opinion still matters.
Then by accident I am not even
master of myself. I slink about
looking for commands and
try to obey. Then reclining
I lose my legs. Now
I am alone. The world streaming
around me.

I find myself
in a field of flowers,

songs from voices I don't know.
Then even knowing is stolen away.

Why? Why did I come here for
such a quick visit?

The Journal of the Future

Yes,
he talks about the truth
as if he owns it,
the voice of discovery.
And it is terrifying,
enough to generate open eyes.

He says,
"Grand things are about
to dwarf our living miracles,
interrupt our peace."
He jumps in glee, book in his hand,
preparing the news for you.

He says,
"Come and behold.
Meet my smile.
Finally lift the darkness."

I resume
my interrupted
laugh.

The Order of Blankets

I never had to worry
about this before. But
now I have a private
science of blankets.
As I get cold I have to
apply my principles of design.
The climate here
is cold in March.

I like the satiny one
against my body,
Pulled up tight around my chin.
The thick fuzziness of wool
on top of that and a layer
of colorful fabric icing
like a cake. I lay, looking
as a human confection,
reaching for a state of zero.

Ear Hands

When I approach the podium
I can see the restlessness
as an idea breathes. I know
how it will be embodied.
The air will lift the weight
in lobes of time. It will be
an invisible dance carried
by moving hands.
Only thin time will lift its weight.
None of us know how. But
as it emerges
some kind of eyes make bodies.

The Ballerina and the Art of Trying

It is clear
they will never achieve their aims.
They reach upward
outward for something
beyond the curve of their hands,
hands that aspire to grace beyond their bodies.
We greet their aspirations with joy and hope.
They nearly do it.
It's all they can make their tenderness do.
Here we see their limits,
fragility, aspiration.
We hope with them. We cheer them.
We urge them on.

The Hero of Ballet

The music I play
is a snob.
I chase away ordinary pleasures
and think it makes me purer.
You will laugh when you see me
standing like a ballet hero
with my ugly human knees.

Watching a Man Grow Old

As far as I can tell
it's difference between the outside
and the in. We are partly blind to changes in ourselves
even if everyone else can see them.
We start to walk and talk differently,
usually you can at least partly see that.
And time splits off into sections of
being here and not. We get partly
cut away, even while we seem to many
to be still alive. Death is part of growth.
It's segmented much the same.
You can keep your eyes as long as you don't close them.
Hope doesn't go away but the roadway to tomorrow
roughens. It's easy. One can see
how the list of places and paths to
love quickly narrow to the closing.

Occasional Appetite

Sometimes my hand seeks flesh
which is scarce in my world.
It has always been so,
except briefly, briefly for
those memories.
Flesh is priveledge,
guarded by ancient laws
that seperate its parts.
Sometimes my hand seeks flesh
through the void,
in the wilderness,
even as the darkness looms.

Development of a Kink

In this case,
accepting the gift
is the greater gift
as judged in the great
hierarchy of gifts.
The winner of the contest
stands proud and the loser
examines himself,
a little abashed.
Another battle passed
and both opponents left a stage
in good health, but the wounds
were deep.

www.ingramcontent.com/pod-product-compliance
Lightning Source LLC
LaVergne TN
LVHW040930150826
845672LV00007B/2286